The Sea Serpent and Me

For Milo, who started out little
and insisted on growing

–D.S.

For my sister, Louise, who is my best friend,
and for my beautiful niece Natalie

–C.C.

All rights reserved. For information about permission to reproduce
selections from this book, write to Permissions, Houghton Mifflin
Company, 215 Park Avenue South, New York, New York 10003.

www.houghtonmifflinbooks.com

The text of this book is set in Egyptienne.
The illustrations are acrylic and charcoal pencil.

Library of Congress Cataloging-in-Publication Data

Slater, Dashka.
The sea serpent and me / written by Dashka Slater and illustrated by
Catia Chien.
p. cm.
Summary: One day a small sea serpent falls from the faucet into the
tub as a child is about to take a bath, and as the days go by and the ser-
pent grows, they both realize that he needs to go back to the sea where
he belongs.
ISBN-13: 978-0-618-72394-2 (hardcover)
ISBN-10: 0-618-72394-3 (hardcover)
[1. Sea monsters—Fiction. 2. Growth—Fiction.] I. Chien, Catia, ill. II.
Title.
PZ7.S62897Se 2008
[E]—dc22

2007015577

Printed in the U.S.A.
WOZ 10 9 8 7 6 5 4 3 2

The Sea Serpent and Me

By

DASHKA SLATER

Illustrated by

CATIA CHIEN

HOUGHTON MIFFLIN COMPANY

BOSTON

On Tuesday, as I was about to climb into the bath, a sea serpent dropped out of the faucet and into the tub.

He was a very beautiful sea serpent,
so small I could hold him in my hands.

In the bath, we played together.
I made the soap dish be a Viking ship,
and he knocked it over with his tail.
Then we made waves and splashed
each other until water covered the floor.

When it was time to get out, I scooped him up and put him in the fish tank next to my bed.

"How did you get here?" I asked him that night. "Don't sea serpents belong in the sea?"

He told me a tornado had lifted him into the clouds one day.

The clouds drifted over green jungles

and silvery cities

and then rained him down into a lake,
where a pipe sucked him up
and whooshed him along
and splashed him down into my tub.

"Do you miss the sea?" I asked him.
"Of course I do. I belong there."
"Then I'll take you back," I said.

But it was rainy on Wednesday,
too rainy for the beach.
My sea serpent was sulky.

"Sea serpents belong in the sea," he said.
"We'll try again tomorrow," I promised.
"But for today, the house can be the beach."

Later, we went swimming in the bathtub,
but it suddenly felt crowded.
"I think you're growing," I said.
He smiled. "Of course I am," he said.
"Once I was as small as a drop of rain.
Soon I'll be as big as a wave."

That night as I lay in bed he sang
me a song about the deep blue sea,

where manta rays swim like dancing blankets

and there are crabs with antlers

and fish shaped like guitars.

On Thursday, it was still raining,
and my sea serpent had grown.
"How big do sea serpents
get?" I asked him.

"We get as big as the ocean is deep,
and as long as the current is strong.
The big ones are as big
as a very small island;
the small ones are as big as a whale."

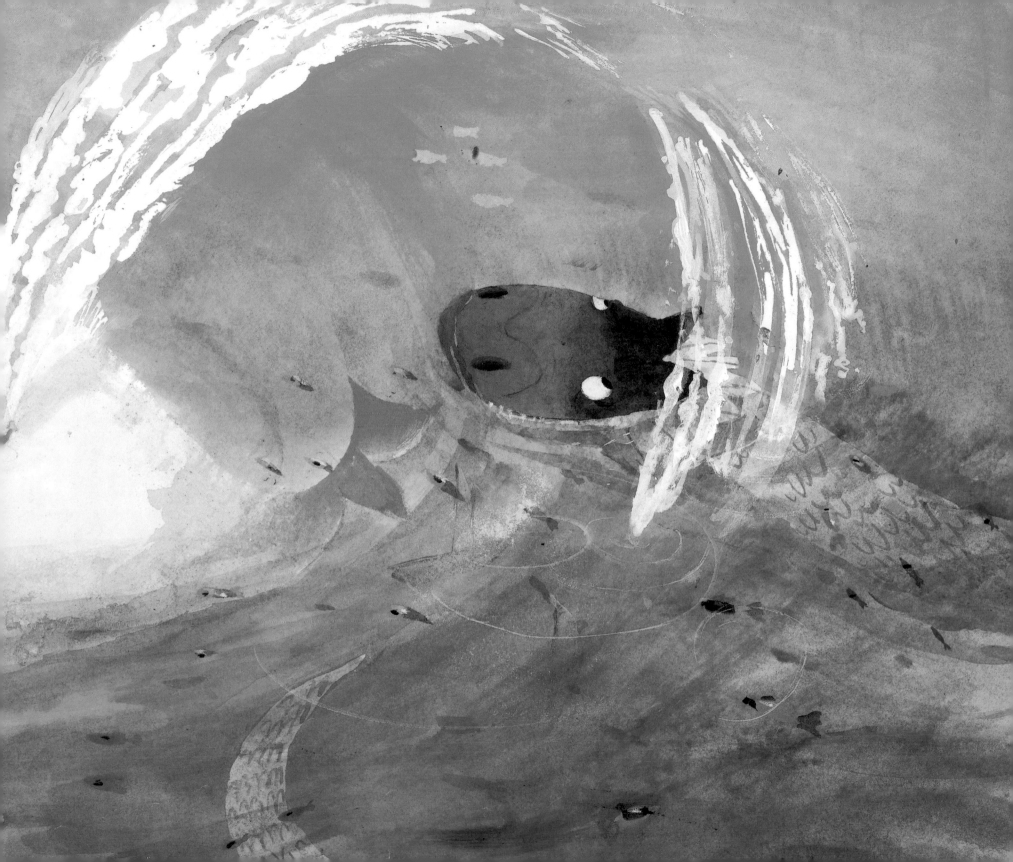

"Oh," I said. "*That* big."

By bedtime, my sea serpent was too large
for the fish tank, so I put him back in the tub.
"I wish I could still sleep next to your bed,"
he said when I kissed him good night.

That night I
heard him singing
his song about the creatures
of the deep blue sea,
and I sort of wanted it to be
sunny in the morning
and I sort of wanted it
to rain.

When Friday came, it was still raining
and my sea serpent was so long
that his tail was resting in the sink.
"If you get any bigger I won't be able to
carry you to the beach," I told him.
"When you think about it," he answered,
"the rain isn't any wetter than the ocean."
"Oh," I said. "Good point."

So I brought him down to the windy shore
and dragged him through the sand
until the water lapped my toes.

My sea serpent dove in
and came up splashing.
"Look how big I am!" he yelled.
"I can touch the bottom with my tail!"

"You're very big," I said, remembering
how I used to hold him in my hands.

Then the sun came out and we swam together.

We rode the waves as if they were horses

and
floated
as
gently
as
stars
in
the
sky.

But people need towels, and dry clothes, and dinner,
and sea serpents belong in the sea.
"I guess it's time to say goodbye," I said
when the sun sank low and pink in the sky.
My sea serpent looked at the great green ocean
that stretched way out to the edge of the world.

"I'm very big," he said. "But the sea's a lot
bigger. Maybe I should stay with you."
I stroked his neck and almost said yes.
But soon he'd be as big as a wave,
and I knew he'd be happiest in the sea.
"I'll stay right here," I told him.
"I'll wait till you're ready."

My sea serpent swam in the shallow water
and I stayed beside him and talked about
manta rays like dancing blankets
and crabs with antlers and fish shaped like guitars.

"You'll have adventures," I said.
"You'll see shipwrecks and sharks,
and schools of fish
like bouquets of flowers."

"But what if I'm lonely?" my sea serpent asked.

"You won't be lonely.

You'll play with sea lions and otters.

Whales will sing with you,

and when you're tired, the waves will rock you to sleep."

"Remember when I was little?" he asked.

"How I slept in a fish tank next to your bed?"

"Of course I do," I said. "You snored."

My sea serpent smiled.

"I'm not so little anymore," he said.

And then he added, "I'm ready to go."

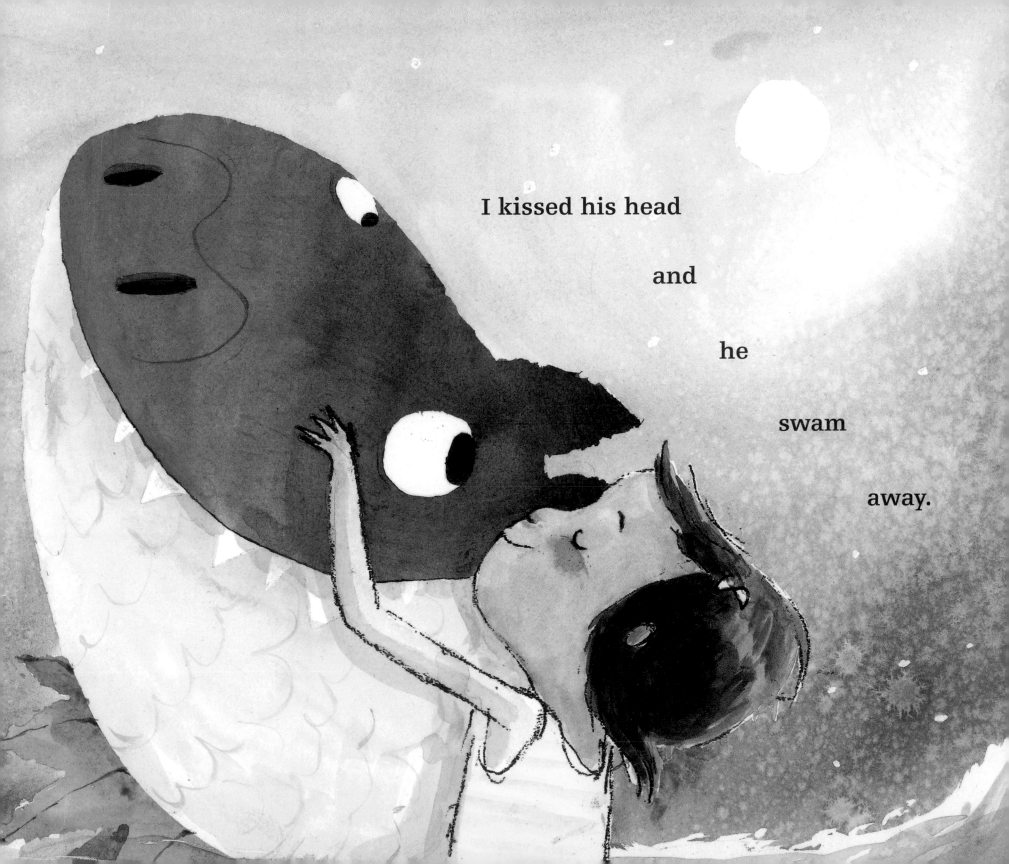

I kissed his head

and

he

swam

away.

That night I opened my window
and listened for the sea.
I could hear the waves, and the laugh of a gull,
and I thought I could hear my sea serpent singing.
So I listened until I fell asleep.